Angels at Work
Elementary Version

Dr. Carolyn Duncan Cecil, D. Min.
Illustrated by Susan Bradbury

Copyright © 2025 by Carolyn Duncan Cecil

All rights reserved. No part of this publication may be reproduced, distributed, or transmitted in any form or by any means, including, photocopying,recording, or other electronic or mechanical methods, without the prior written permission of the copyright owner and the publisher, except in the case of brief quotations embodied in critical reviews and certain other noncommercial uses permitted by copyright law. For permission requests, write to the publisher, addressed "Attention: Permissions Coordinator," at the address below.

ARPress
45 Dan Road Suite 5
Canton MA 02021

Hotline: 1(888) 821-0229
Fax: 1(508) 545-7580

Ordering Information:
Quantity sales. Special discounts are available on quantity purchases by corporations, associations, and others. For details, contact the publisher at the address above.

Printed in the United States of America.

ISBN-13: Paperback   979-8-89676-330-7
              eBook   979-8-89676-331-4

Library of Congress Control Number: 2025904626

God's Secret Agents

Some learn about angels from the Bible, a church, pastor, or friend,
God made all the angels, and the Holy ones work for Him.

An encounter with an angel is like nothing you have seen,
Some shine like a rainbow or a brilliant color gleam.

Angel means messenger or agent, sometimes used to intervene,
Think of them as secret agents, because angels remain unseen.

There are many ranks of angels and names of the Heavenly Hosts:
Sons of God, Holy Ones, and Morning Stars, not to boast.

God's angels are so big, and they are mighty and strong,
They watch over the children, and protect them all day long.

Even though we cannot see them, they are really here,
Singing songs of joy, over all the children held so dear.

Angels are not bound by walls or limited by time and space,
So, they will be there when you call, anytime and anyplace.

From north to south and east to west, angels come and go,
They spend their time helping us and fighting every foe.

Angel Protection
(Psalm 91:11)

When Daniel was thrown in the lion's den, God had a plan,
An angel shut the lion's mouth because Daniel was an innocent man.
(Dan. 6:22)

Three men who worshipped God were thrown in a furnace by the King,
A fourth appeared with them in the flames, and they didn't burn a thing.
(Daniel 3:19-25)

Psalm 91:11 says God gave "angels charge over us,"
Not as rulers or our leaders, but as protectors we can trust!

That verse says angels "will keep us, in all of our ways,"
Ask for angel protection to help you all your days.

Ask God to send angels to your school and the playground too,
Or quote a scripture verse, and ask the angels to move for you!
(Psalm 103:20)

When you hear about terrible tornados, hurricanes, and floods,
Ask for angels to fly real fast and help them out of the mud!

Angels are watching you at school and protecting you at play,
Angels are listening to everything, so be careful what you say.

If people realized that angels were watching all day through,
They would probably change the kind of things they say and often do!

Angels All Around

Every time you take a road trip, angels are all around,
On the right, left, front, and back, holy angels do surround.

They are faster than the wind, faster than a blink,
In a nanosecond they can move anywhere you think.

Some angels look like rainbows, some like fire and flames,
When they scoot across the sky, a streak of orange remains.
(Revelation 10:1)

Angels take your breath away; being in their presence is intense,
But do not bow down and worship them, it causes God offense.
(Colossians 2:18; Revelation 22:8-9)

Angels can know the future and know about human prayer,
They have emotions like joy and love; feelings we all share.
(Luke 1:13-16; Luke 2:13-14)

When angels appear to people, they often say, "Fear Not!"
Encountering an angel can put us in a scary spot.

God's throne room is filled with glory, power, light, and fire,
And millions of angels praise Him in a continuous heavenly choir.
(Daniel 7:9-10)

In the throne room Our God shines like jasper, sardis, and emerald,
Seven lamps, lightning, thunder, voices, and angels are assembled.
(Rev. 4:3)

Angels Love to Travel

Angels are at the airport, just imagine a big angel on each wing,
When that airplane takes off, no one will see a thing.

Angels are at the bus station, and they like to go on trips,
They ride on top the bus, so the big bus will not tip!

Angels love to travel on rockets and they really like the train,
Where they sing "Holy, Holy, Holy is our Lord," in a continuous refrain!

If you go on a boat ride, they will be there too,
They will ride ships or canoes just to be with you.

In an eighteen wheeler, motorcycle, van, truck, or car,
Angels will ride on anything because it is you they guard.

You are the apple of His eye; your name is written on His palm,
God sends angels to guard you, because He thinks you're the bomb.
(Zechariah 2:8; Isaiah 49:16)

God created you, and He designed you to go travel,
But an angel must go with you, so things will not unravel.

If you traveled in a space craft all the way to the space station,
An angel would travel with you to get you to your destination.

Angels Want to do Stuff

An angel needs a prayer, a scripture or angelic work orders,
Don't let your angels sit around getting bored at Angel Headquarters.

Angels listen to the voice of God, so ask Him to send them today,
Quote scripture or say your prayers to get those angels on their way!
(Psalm 103:20-21)

The Bible says there are angels known as ministering spirits,
They minister to seekers and children when they need it.
(Heb.1:14)

If someone gets sick, you can ask for angels too,
To fight for their recovery or help them when they're blue.

An angel's most important job is what they were designed to do,
They praise, worship, and bless the Lord, until each day is through.
(Psalm 148:1-2)

God wants us to dance and sing, and praise Him with our whole being,
And very soon His many blessings we will surely be seeing.
(Psalm 149)

Lord Holy Spirit uses angels to bring seekers to re-birth,
So, angels are working everywhere in all the nations of this Earth.

Our God is in a good mood; He throws no lightning bolts,
But He wants the best for all, which is what His Word promotes.

More Angel Facts

Jacob saw multitudes of angels ascending a ladder in a dream,
Did he discover the gate of heaven? To him that's how it seemed.
(Genesis 28:12)

How many angels are there? Myriads and myriads the Bible says,
Myriads means "too many to be counted," the dictionary says.
(Revelation 5:11)

How many angels fit in God's big heavenly Throne Room?
Ten thousand times ten thousand, plus more angels we presume!
(Revelation 5:11)

Angels "excel in strength" and are sent to "do God's Word,"
Like them we should heed God's voice and do what we have heard.
(Psalm 103:20)

Humans have entertained angels, thinking they were strangers,
Mighty angels have delivered people from many terrible dangers.
(Heb.13:2)

Angels and humans can rebel; it does not make our God happy,
It would be best to turn around and not hurt our Heavenly Pappy.
(1 Samuel 15:23)

From birth until they guide you to heaven, your angel will be there,
God cherishes all His children, and these angels show His care.

"Then he dreamed, and behold, a ladder was set up on the earth, and its top reached to heaven; and there the angels of God were ascending and descending on it…"
Genesis 28:12 NKJV

Angels Proclaimed the Birth of Christ

Gabriel announced Mary's pregnancy, and said "call His name JESUS,"
He was born when Mary and Joseph were in Bethlehem for the census.
                                                  (Luke 1:31; Luke 2:21)

Gabriel's message said: "Of His Kingdom there will be no end,"
"He will be great...called the Son of the Highest." He will be our friend.
                                                  (Luke 1:32-33)

Mary "brought forth her firstborn Son, and...laid him in a manger,
Across the region, this event was described in detail by an angel.
                                                  (Luke 2:7)

Angels came to the shepherds, watching their flocks by night,
A multitude of heavenly hosts came and it was a glorious sight!
                                                  (Luke 2:8; Luke 2:13)

"I bring you good tidings of great joy..." an angel then assured,
"For there is born to you this day... a Savior who is Christ the Lord.'
                                                  (Luke 2:10)

"Glory to God in the highest and on earth peace, good will to men,"
The angel choir sang over and over in exalted honor of Him.
                                                  (Luke 2:14)

After hearing from the angels, the shepherds went to see,
They found the family just as told and made it known widely.

Holy Warrior Angels

Warrior angels protect your home, school, work, and family,
You can always count on God to send angels to fight for thee.

If you get sick, holy angel warriors will surely fight for you,
They will run those bad guys off, just ask for an angel or two.

If you go to Sunday school, church, or special studies,
Ask God to send warriors to guard you and all your buddies.

Ask God to put a warrior on the roof and one out in the yard,
So, you can go to sleep in peace; they are powerful in that regard.

Two praying in agreement can put ten thousand angels to flight,
Some Christians don't even ask for one to help fight the good fight.
                                    (Deuteronomy 32:30; 1 Timothy 1:18)

Angel armies have praise on their lips and swords in their hands,
Praise cuts through the enemy lines and stops the bad guy's plans.

Matthew 16:27 says warrior angels will come back with the Son,
And everyone will be rewarded for the things that they have done.

All the people in the Lamb's Book of Life will get to go to heaven,
Warrior angels will escort all and get them to their destination.

"For the Son of Man is going to come in the glory of His Father with His angels and will then repay every man according to his deeds."

Matthew 12:7 NASB

Michael, the Warrior Archangel

The beautiful name of *Michael* means "who is like God,"
We are awed by his celestial beauty, yet he is God's lightning-rod.

Michael is an archangel, a warrior of the highest angel position,
It seems nothing can stop him when he is on a mission.
                                                               (Jude 9)

Michael is one of the mightiest warrior angels of them all,
He will fight and show his strength when he hears the call.

Daniel's words were heard from the first moment of his prayers,
But until Angel Michael came to help, it appeared that no one cared.
                                                          (Dan. 10:13)

Michael is Prince over the nation Israel and a mighty defender too,
At his command, millions of angels will do what he says to do.
                                                          (Dan. 10:21)

Revelation 12 says that Michael will wage war with the dragon,
The dragon is the devil and there is no place for him in heaven.
                                     (Revelation 12:7; 20:1-3, 7-10)

He will fight evil angels until the Lord's Kingdom comes,
He will fight until the glory light shines down on everyone.

The archangel Michael is in first place, so he is number one,
But Gabriel is the messenger, faster than fast; he will not be out done.

"And war broke out in heaven: Michael and his angels fought with the dragon; and the dragon and his angels fought, but they did not prevail, nor was a place found for them in heaven any longer." **Revelation 12:7 NKJV**

Gabriel and the Messenger Angels

Gabriel the messenger angel is mighty, strong, and fast,
He can get a message out; for Gabriel it is not a task.

Gabriel's name means "hero of God" but he is a hero to us all,
He can deliver a message whenever he hears God's call.

Gabriel stands in the presence of God, very near the throne,
Gabriel is always waiting there for a message he can make known.

Sometimes Gabriel gets so near the Throne, his face shines like the sun,
He is as bright as a shooting star that passes over everyone.

The Old Testament tells us Gabriel went to visit Daniel twice,
He gave him messages about the latter days, full of good advice.
(Dan. 8:15; 9:21)

One time it took twenty-one days for a Messenger to break through,
An evil prince of Persia kept that Angel from doing what he had to do.
(Dan. 10:6)

Gabriel announced to Zechariah the birth of John the Baptist,
He would be filled with the Holy Spirit and everything they wished.
(Luke 1:15-19)

Gabriel went to Nazareth to tell Mary she would be a mother,
Her Son was to become our Savior; He would be like no other!
(Luke 1:26-33)

"And the angel answered and said to him, I am Gabriel, who stands in the presence of God, and was sent to speak to you and bring you these glad tidings."

Luke 1:19 NKJV

Seraphim

The prophet Isaiah said the seraphim angels have three sets of wings:
Two cover their face, two their feet, and two make them flying beings.
(Isaiah 6)

Seraphim angels are beautiful, burning, fiery, and take your breath away
They glide across the firmament in a translucent orange display.

Yellow, orange, and red; seraphim glow like flames that never die,
When they take off, they make a fiery orange streak across the sky.

Heavenly beings, called seraphim, praise God around His throne,
They are so devoted to Him that they stay in their sanctuary home.
(Isaiah 6)

Seraphim stay close to the throne and worship God always,
Above the throne a rainbow gleams in emerald light arrays.
(Isaiah 6; Revelation 4:3)

To the Heavenly Father they sing "*Holy, holy, holy is the Lord of hosts,*"
"*The whole earth is full of His glory,*" the seraphim gloriously boast.
(Isaiah 6:3)

Revelation 5:11 says ten thousand angels times ten thousand more,
Fill the throne room and sing to the Lamb that they adore.
(Revelation 5:11)

Living creatures, elders, and angels are there singing a new song,
"*Worthy is the Lamb who was slain*" is sung by this mighty throng.
(Revelation 5:12)

"Above it stood seraphim; each one had six wings: with two he covered his face, with two he covered his feet, and with two he flew." Isaiah 6:2 NKJV

Cherubim

Cherubim are a high class of beings, found on the sides of the throne,
They are striking and powerful, but their mighty strength is still unknown.

Ezekiel describes the cherubim as complex and amazing beings,
A wheel within a wheel, wings, hands, and many eyes for seeing.
(Ezekiel 10)

Cherubim have four faces: an eagle, lion, calf, and man,
They fly any direction without turning from where they began.

They declare the glory of God and declare His holiness too,
Cherubim sing twenty-four/seven; their song is never through!
(Isaiah 6)

The words they sing all the time are never boring to anyone,
"Holy, Holy, Holy, Lord God Almighty, who was and is and is to come!"
(Rev. 4:6-8)

The cherubim sing out thanks and worship every single hour,
"You are worthy, O Lord, to receive glory and honor and power."
(Rev. 4:6-8)

Cherubim and seraphim worship our God until the whole room is elated,
"For You created all things, And by Your will they exist and were created."

Cherubim see everything and have the most important job,
They are the ones who always surround and guard Almighty God.

"*The first living creature was like a lion, the second living creature was like a calf, the third living creature had the face of a man, and the fourth living creature was like a flying eagle.*"

Revelation 4:7 NKJV

Guarding God's Precious Creation

You are the highest creation that God ever designed,
More valuable than planets and stars and all the rest combined.

What some fail to realize is, we are all trophies of God's creation,
Our worth cannot be measured; all of heaven gave shouts of acclamation.

There was thunderous applause on the day you were created,
You are God's mighty workmanship; a treasure never to be hated.

Angels guard all precious Christians in the morning and evening too,
They will always be on guard; their job is never through!

Guardian angels are not interested in guarding gold and silver,
They are only interested in you, God's most precious treasure!

Guardian angels protect the babies, children, teens, and grown-ups too,
They are serious about their job and they will always see it through.

A child of God will never be left as an orphan in the storm,
The angels will always keep watch, from late night to early morn.

The Lord above is watching over you real close,
Your angels are assigned to you and will not leave their posts.

"Be careful that you do not corrupt one of these little ones. For I can assure you that in heaven each of their angelic guardians have instant access to my heavenly Father."

Matthew 18:10 TPT

An Encouraging Word

After hearing about these angels and how much you are adored,
Maybe you need to decide to make Jesus Christ your Lord.

Jesus did not come to judge us; He came to make a way,
That He could pay for our sin because the devil led us astray.

When you honestly believe, you will get a brand-new start,
He will be by your side, a good brother who will not depart.

As you go through life with the Lord, nothing will be missing,
You will have a purpose and destiny, not just hoping and wishing.
(2 Peter 22:3)

Remember, you are God's trophy; He sees you as a treasure,
And every time He looks at you, you give Him so much pleasure.

Jesus is not going to be happy if one human being is lost,
Tell your friends about the Lord, so they won't have to pay the cost.

If you accept Jesus in your heart, I will see you in heaven,
And we will be friends forever after our earthly session.

The prayer is easy: Jesus, forgive me for my sin, come into my heart,
Help me read your Word and live for you, thank you for new start.

Until We Meet Again...

Angel stories are from the Bible, but there is more to know,
You will learn many more exciting facts, as you continue to grow.

Because you are a Christian, you can send angels to new stations,
Pray they go to help those in trouble all across the nations.

I hope it brought you happiness learning something new,
The Word of God has more exciting things I want to share with you.

The Bible has stories of good and bad, to help with our success,
Read a page or two each day before you lie down to rest.

Until next time we meet again, sharing a book or two,
Be confident in the fact of how much Father God loves you!

Good Night, Precious Child

d's mercy is new every morning, that means you have nothing to fe(
 rest your mind and rest your heart, and tomorrow things will be cle(

member, a child will never be left as an orphan in a storm,
gels will keep watch, from late night to early morn.

e Lord up above is watching...He is guarding you real close,
ver forget your angels are there, stationed at their command posts.

The End,
I love you cherished one!

Other Books by Carolyn Cecil:

Life on Earth, What a Journey
Our Good Earth
Simple Holiday Pleasures
Smells to Treasure
Holy Spirit at Work (Children's Version)
Holy Spirit at Work (For Youth)
Angels at Work (For Youth)

Equipped: Equipping and Empowerment
for Christians and Lay Ministers Vol.1,2,3

www.ingramcontent.com/pod-product-compliance
Lightning Source LLC
Chambersburg PA
CBHW040001040426
42337CB00032B/5181